EVERYDAY SCIENCE

EVERYDAY SCIENCE

Fun and Easy Projects for Making Practical Things

Shar Levine and Leslie Johnstone

John Wiley & Sons, Inc.

New York • **Chichester** • **Brisbane** • **Toronto** • **Singapore**

The publisher and the authors have made every reasonable effort to ensure that the experiments and activities in this book are safe when conducted as instructed but assume no responsibility for any damage caused or sustained while performing the experiments or activities in this book. Parents, guardians, and/or teachers should supervise young readers who undertake the experiments and activities in this book.

Library of Congress Cataloging-in-Publication Data
Levine, Shar.
   Everyday science: fun and easy projects for making practical things/Shar Levine
and Leslie Johnstone.
      p.   cm
   Includes index.
   ISBN 0-471-11014-0 (alk. paper)
      1. Science—Experiments—Popular works.   2. Science—Experiments—Juvenile litera-
   ture.   3. Scientific recreations—Popular works.   4. Scientific recreations—Juvenile literature.
   [1. Science—Experiments.   2. Experiments.   3. Scientific recreations.   4. Games.
   5. Science projects.]   I. Johnstone, Leslie.   II. Title.
   Q164.L473   1995
   507.8—dc20   94-24700
                                                                              AC

To my mother, Dorothy Levine, and as always, to my husband and children, thanks.

Shar

To my parents, Janice and Ron Pickerill, and my sisters, Holly Sharf and Melissa Davidson, for their love and support.

Leslie

Acknowledgments

We would like to thank Kate Bradford for her encouragement, advice, and support.

CONTENTS

INTRODUCTION

Look around you. Science is everywhere. When you turn on a light, watch television, or answer a phone, you are influenced by science. Everyday things that we take for granted would have seemed like magic to people 50 years ago. Fax machines, laptop computers, and cellular phones are some recent science inventions. Can you imagine how scientific inventions will affect our lives 50 years from now? Will people have silicon chips placed in their bodies to provide medical information to doctors? Will we travel through phone lines instead of using cars or planes? Will you read a book like this one on a computer in your own home?

This book is designed to help you understand some of the science you use every day. There are 25 different experiments in this book. Each experiment includes a list of materials, a series of easy-to-follow steps, an explanation of the scientific principle demonstrated, and a Did You Know? section that offers additional scientific facts and information on each topic. You should have everything you need to perform the experiments right in your own kitchen, so there is no need to buy special or expensive materials.

HOW TO USE THIS BOOK

Read through each activity before you begin. Gather all the materials before starting, and place them in the order that you will use them. Give yourself plenty of space to work. Science can be messy, so wear old clothes while doing the experiment and cover any surfaces with newspaper. Do not eat, drink, or taste any of the experiments. Keep your work area neat, and wash instruments and hands after performing all activities.

By building and experimenting with these projects, you will learn about the science behind the way ordinary things work. And you'll also discover that science is fun! Remember, many of these activities will make successful science fair projects or even great gifts.

PART I
LIGHT AND OPTICS

CHAPTER 1
SOMEWHERE OVER THE RAINBOW

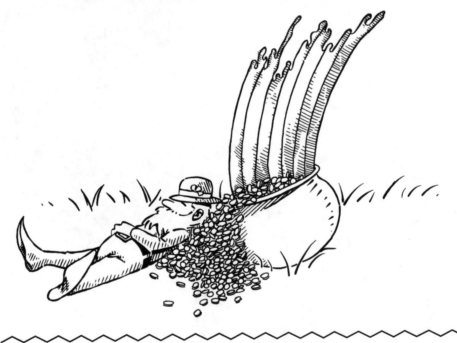

Do you know our friend Mr. Biv? Roy G. Biv is the name used to remember the colors of the rainbow in order from red to violet. Here's a dry way to create your own rainbows!

YOU WILL NEED

scissors

shoe box

white paper

clear drinking glass

tap water

feather

night-light

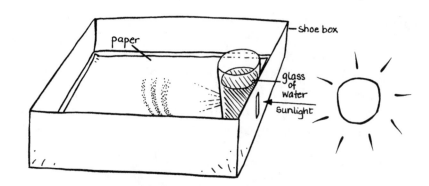

WHAT TO DO

1. Cut a ½-inch (1-cm) slit in one end of the shoe box.

2. Cut the paper to fit the bottom of the box, and place it in the box.

3. In the morning or evening, place the box in a bright window so that sunlight can enter through the slit.

4. Fill the glass with water then place it against the slit and on top of the white paper.

5. Look at the paper.

6. Look with one eye through a bird's feather at a soft light, such as a night-light.

CAUTION: Do not look directly at the sun.

WHAT HAPPENED

The light made rainbows on the paper and in the feather. The light came in through the water or the feather in **waves** (movements that repeat themselves). The light waves were **refracted** (bent) by the water and spread out into a **spectrum**, or rainbow of colors. The different colors were due to the specific **wavelength** (distance between similar points on the wave) of each light wave. Red light has the longest wavelength because it is refracted the least. Violet light has the shortest wavelength because it is refracted the most. The colors of the spectrum, from longest to shortest wavelength, are red, orange, yellow, green, blue, indigo, and violet. The first letter of each color gives the name Roy G. Biv.

DID YOU KNOW?

- Sunlight is made up of different colors. Objects appear to be certain colors because they **reflect** (give back) specific wavelengths of light. Green plants, for example, appear green because they reflect green light. They **absorb** (take in) all light that is not green. Special lights used to grow plants are usually blue or purple. Plants would die if grown under green light, because none of the light would be absorbed.

CHAPTER 2
COLLIDING COLORS

A kaleidoscope is a tube that has a peephole at one end and mirrors and pieces of shiny colored materials at the other end. When the tube is turned, the colored materials tumble and are reflected in the mirrors. There are many different kinds of kaleidoscopes sold in stores today. Some have beautiful cases, some have multi-faceted lenses, and others have marbles at the end. Little did Sir David Brewster realize when he invented the kaleidoscope in the early 1800s that this toy would become so popular.

YOU WILL NEED

8-by-8-inch (20-by-20-cm) sheet of thick black cardboard

8-by-8-inch (20-by-20-cm) sheet of aluminum foil

scissors

glue

tape

clear plastic wrap

bits of colored cellophane, Mylar, or sparkles

translucent balloon (available from many specialty balloon stores)

WHAT TO DO

1. Fold the cardboard in half, then in half again in the same direction. You now have a piece of cardboard with four long panels of the same size.

2. Place the foil, shiny side up, on top of the cardboard and fold back one end of the foil so that one of the panels is uncovered. Trim the foil along this fold.

3. Glue the foil to three of the panels.

4. Fold the cardboard so that the foil-covered panels face each other and the folds come together.

5. Tape the uncovered panel to the back of one of the foil-covered panels. If the foil-covered panels do not lie flat and at angles to each other, secure them with a small piece of tape.

6. Cover both ends of the cardboard with clear plastic wrap, and tape the wrap to the panels.

7. Cut small bits of colored cellophane or Mylar, and place them inside the balloon. Add sparkles to the balloon. Do not add too many bits, or the light won't shine through.

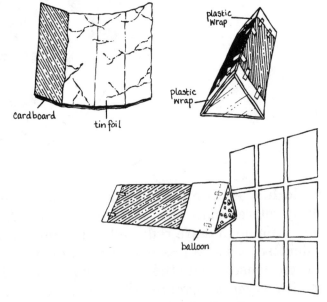

cardboard tin foil plastic wrap plastic wrap balloon

8. Cut the mouthpiece off the balloon, and slide the balloon opening over one end of the cardboard. Adjust the balloon so that it is flat across the end of the cardboard. Tape the balloon in place.

9. Hold your kaleidoscope up to a window and look through the end opposite the balloon. Turn the kaleidoscope to see the different patterns the objects make.

NOTE: You can use real mirrors instead of aluminum foil. Ask a glass cutter to cut three mirrors that are just slightly smaller than the foil-covered panels. Be sure to have the glass cutter grind the edges of the glass so that there are no sharp edges. Glue the mirrors in place as you did in step 3 above.

WHAT HAPPENED

You created a kaleidoscope. The shiny surface of foil or mirrors reflected the colored bits of cellophane and Mylar. Because there were three shiny surfaces, they reflected not only the colored bits but also each other's images. This created the multiple patterns that you saw. A **scope** is any device that is used to look at things. Many other objects that you look through have *scope* as part of their name.

DID YOU KNOW?

- When you look at yourself in the mirror, you don't see yourself as other people see you. What you see is your **mirror image**, a reverse copy of yourself. Try holding this page up to the mirror. The words are not the same in the mirror as they are on this page. Can you write a message that can only be read in a mirror? It makes a neat secret code!

- Leonardo da Vinci (1452–1519), the famous artist and scientist, used mirror writing to record his observations in his diary.

9

CHAPTER 3
MOVIE MAGIC

Would you like to make cartoons when you grow up? Why wait that long? Here's how you can animate your drawings and entertain your friends and family right now. Zoetropes and praxinoscopes are similar types of moving picture machines. A **zoetrope** is a device shaped like a cylinder with a slit in one side through which a series of pictures can be viewed, while a **praxinoscope** uses mirrors to reflect drawings that are on the inside of a drum. In this experiment, you will make a zoetrope.

YOU WILL NEED

NOTE: A simple zoetrope can be made by **recycling** (reusing rather than throwing away) an old spinning top. Look around the house or check garage sales to see if you can find the type of top that sticks to the floor with a suction cup and is spun by pumping a knob at the end of a spiraling plunger.

old spinning top with a footed base

or

    deep round baking pan or cookie tin

    modeling clay (plasticine)

    marble

    dart with suction cup

scissors

cardboard

pencil, nail, or skewer (to be used only by an adult)

tape measure

paper

ruler

colored pencils or felt-tip pens

transparent tape

adult helper

WHAT TO DO

1. If you are not using a spinning top, make a zoetrope this way:

- Turn the pan upside down. Place a small amount of modeling clay (plasticine) in the middle of the bottom of the pan.

- Firmly push the marble into the modeling clay so that the marble forms a round surface that the pan can spin on.

- Turn the pan over. Suction the dart to the center of the inside bottom of the pan. The dart will be used to spin the pan.

2. Make the viewer.

- Cut a piece of cardboard that is about the same size as a postcard.

- Have an adult use a pencil to poke a small peephole in the center of the card.

3. Make the cartoon.

- To measure the strip of paper for the cartoon, wrap the tape measure around the circumference (widest round part) of the top or pan. Cut a strip of paper 2 to 3 inches (5 to 7.5 cm) wide and as long as the measurement shown on the tape measure.

- Use the ruler to divide the strip of paper into a single row of 10 to 12 blocks of equal size. These blocks will be called frames.

- Color a simple figure in the first frame. In the next frame, use the same figure, but change the position of one part just slightly. After the fifth or sixth frame, the figure in the remaining frames should gradually return to the position in the first frame. This will make the pictures flow together smoothly in a repeating loop when viewed.

4. When you have finished making the cartoon, tape the strip of paper to the circumference of the zoetrope.

5. Spin the zoetrope, and watch the drawings through the peephole.

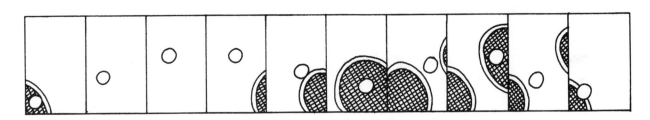

WHAT HAPPENED

When you watched the drawings through the peephole, the pictures seemed to come to life. The frames were spinning so fast that they created an **optical illusion** (a misleading visual image). Your eyes saw the individual pictures, but the message of each picture went to your brain so fast that your brain interpreted them as a single, moving picture.

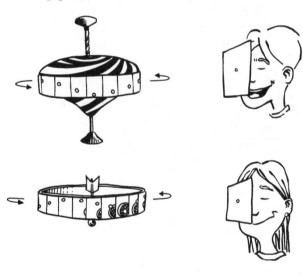

DID YOU KNOW?

- When you watch a television show or a movie in which the wheels of a car, bicycle, or wagon are turning, it sometimes looks as though they are standing still or turning backward. This is because movies, much like a zoetrope, are a sequence of frames. About 24 different frames are shown per second. If the spokes of the wheels are changing position at the same speed as the frames, they appear to be standing still. At other speeds, the wheels appear to be turning either backward or forward. This appearance of stopping or slowing the movement of turning objects is called the **stroboscopic effect**.

CHAPTER 4
SAY CHEESE

Here's how you can make your own camera, then use it to take a real picture. Picture yourself showing off your new homemade camera to your friends.

YOU WILL NEED

round can (such as an empty oatmeal container or coffee can with opaque plastic lid)

pencil

black construction paper

scissors

glue

nail (to be used only by an adult)

transparent tape

aluminum foil

dressmaker's pin

bandage

several empty matchboxes

red cellophane or acrylic

flashlight

unexposed black-and-white 35 mm film

chair

timer

heavy black plastic bag

adult helper

WHAT TO DO

To Make the Camera:

1. Line the inside of the can with the construction paper.

   • To line the bottom of the can, trace a circle around the bottom of the can on the paper. Cut out the circle. Trim the paper a little if necessary for a good fit, then glue it to the inside bottom of the can.

   • To line the sides of the can, wrap the paper around the can, and cut it to the size of the can. Trim the paper if necessary, then glue it to the inside of the can.

2. Have an adult poke a small hole in the bottom of the can with a nail. Make sure the hole goes through the paper that lines the bottom of the can.

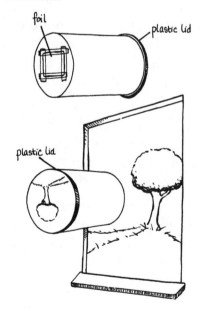

foil

plastic lid

plastic lid

3. Tape a small piece of aluminum foil over the hole, then carefully pierce the foil once with a dress-maker's pin.

4. Place the lid on the can.

5. To see whether your camera works, turn the lights off and point the hole end of the camera toward the window. You should see whatever object is outside the window reflected on the plastic lid. Don't be surprised if the image is upside down!

To Take a Picture:

1. Cover the hole with a bandage so that the light will not enter the camera until you are ready. This is called the shutter because it shuts out light.

2. Glue several matchboxes to one side of the outside of the can so that the can does not roll when placed on a flat surface.

3. Wrap red cellophane around the beam end of a flashlight, and secure it with tape. The flashlight will be called the safe light because it will not expose film but will help you to see what you are doing in the dark.

4. Turn on the safe light, then darken the room by turning off all the lights and closing the curtains.

5. Remove the roll of film from its canister. Using the plastic lid of the camera as a guide, cut a piece of film slightly shorter than the lid. Return the unused film to its canister.

6. Remove the lid from your camera, then tape the film to the inside of the lid by placing tape along the perforated edges of the film. The emulsion (dull) side of the film should be facing you. Carefully replace the lid on the camera so that no light can enter.

7. Turn on the lights, and turn off the safe light. Take the camera out-doors and point it at the object you wish to take a picture of. You have to leave your camera in one place for several minutes to get a good picture. It is hard to hold a camera perfectly still for that long, so place it on a chair, table, or other flat surface.

8. Holding the camera still with one hand, carefully open the shutter by removing the bandage. Leave the shutter open for 5 minutes on a sunny day, 10 minutes on a cloudy day, and 15 minutes on a really cloudy day. After that time, close the shutter by holding the camera still and replacing the bandage. Take the camera indoors.

9. Turn on the safe light, and darken the room. Remove the exposed film from the lid of the camera, and place it in a heavy black plastic bag. Take the bag to a photo store for processing (developing and printing), or store the bag in a drawer until you are ready to have the film processed.

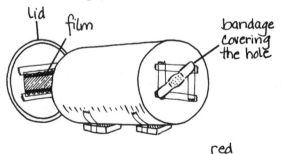

WHAT HAPPENED

You made a **camera obscura.** In a camera obscura, light enters through a pinhole, which acts as a **lens** (curved piece of clear glass or other transparent material) to focus an object. An image of the object is projected upside down on a screen at the other end of the camera. The screen in your camera was the lid. When you put film on this screen, the image was projected on the film, and the camera became a **pinhole camera**. Photographic film has a light-sensitive layer, called the emulsion, that reacts to light. The bright areas of the object reflected more light than the shaded areas, so the film reacted more to the bright areas. After processing, the film became what is called a negative because the bright areas of the object appeared dark. When a light was shone through the negative, the dark sections let less light pass through, so a positive (true) image was produced.

DID YOU KNOW?

- The emulsion side of film and paper is made of a mixture of metallic salt called silver bromide and a jellylike substance called gelatin. The silver bromide turns to silver when it is exposed to light. The tiny silver particles look black. Any leftover silver bromide that isn't used in processing reacts with a chemical called fixative so that it can be rinsed away. Many photographic laboratories recycle the silver left over from the discarded fixative and paper. One lake in Ontario, Canada was so **polluted** (poisoned) with industrial byproducts that film could be developed with the water from it without adding any chemicals.

CHAPTER 5
I CAN SEE FOR MILES AND MILES

A **telescope** is an instrument that is used for getting a closer view of distant objects by **magnifying** (enlarging) the images of objects. **Astronomical** telescopes are used for looking at stars and planets, while **terrestrial** telescopes magnify objects on Earth. Some telescopes show things right side up, while others show things upside down. With a few inexpensive store-bought lenses, you can build your own telescope.

YOU WILL NEED

2 plastic or glass magnifying lenses of different size

modeling clay (plasticine)

wooden ruler

paper

pencil

WHAT TO DO

1. Determine each lens's **focal length** (distance from a lens to the point where the image of an object can be focused).

   • Use a blob of modeling clay to attach the larger lens to the outer edge of one end of the ruler. Do not cover the measurement marks with the clay. Place the clay at the end of the ruler where the lower numbers begin.

   • With the free end of the ruler near you, point the lens toward a small window. Hold a sheet of paper perpendicular to the ruler, and move it closer to or farther from the lens until you can see the image of the window clearly on the paper. The mark on the ruler under the paper is the focal length of the lens. Record this measurement, and remove the lens.

   • Repeat the procedure for the smaller lens, but do not remove it after recording the measurement.

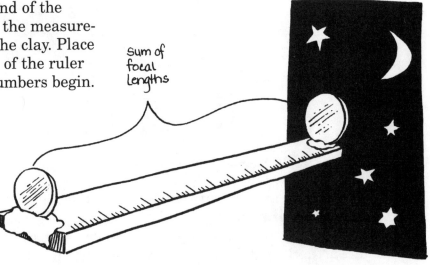

sum of focal lengths

2. Add the focal length of the two lenses.

3. Place another blob of modeling clay on the ruler, positioning it over the mark that is equal to the sum of the two focal lengths. Mount the larger lens on this blob.

4. Point the ruler toward an object, and look through the smaller lens. If the object is out of focus, make a slight adjustment of the position of the larger lens.

5. Use your telescope on a clear night to look at planets and stars.

WARNING: Do not look directly at the sun!

WHAT HAPPENED

You made a **refracting telescope**. This type of telescope uses lenses that refract light and produce an upside-down image. The image made by the larger lens in your telescope was very small, so the smaller lens magnified it, but the image was still upside down. **Astronomers** (scientists who study objects in the sky) use **reflecting telescopes**, which are made of curved mirrors that not only focus light but also flip the image right side up.

DID YOU KNOW?

- Astronomers believe they have found planets outside our Solar System. They have made this discovery through the use of special telescopes called **radio telescopes**. These huge telescopes, which look like satellite dishes, pick up **radio waves** coming from space. Radio waves are waves of energy that can only be picked up by radio receivers. Radio waves can occur naturally, like those given off by the sun or other stars, or they can be produced artificially, like those used to transmit radio broadcasts. Research scientists looking for life on other planets monitor the sky for radio waves that have patterns. One such group of scientists is called SETI, which stands for Search for Extraterrestrial Intelligence.

PART II
HEAT

CHAPTER 6
A THIN RED LINE

A **thermometer** is an instrument that is used to measure temperature. In some countries, people measure temperature in Fahrenheit. In this scale, named after the German scientist Gabriel Fahrenheit, water freezes at 32 degrees and boils at 212 degrees. In other countries, people measure temperature in Celsius, where water freezes at 0 degrees and boils at 100 degrees. The Celsius scale was named after the Swedish scientist Anders Celsius. No matter which scale you use to make your homemade thermometer, this experiment will measure up to all your expectations.

YOU WILL NEED

drill or nail (to be used only by an adult)

small, clear glass bottle with cork stopper

long, thin clear plastic straw or glass tube

modeling clay (plasticine) (optional)

rubbing alcohol

food coloring

masking tape

thick piece of paper

indoor thermometer

2 pans—one filled with ice water, the other filled with hot water

pen or pencil

adult helper

WHAT TO DO

1. Have an adult drill a hole in the cork big enough for the straw to fit through. Do not worry if the hole is too big, as you can seal the hole later with modeling clay.

2. Gently push the straw through the hole so that one end of the straw reaches the bottom of the bottle while the other end extends at least 6 inches (15 cm) beyond the end of the cork. If there is too much space around the straw in the cork, place plasticine around the opening.

3. Fill the bottle full with rubbing alcohol, and add a few drops of food coloring.

4. Gently place the straw and cork in the bottle and close.

5. Tape the paper to the side of the bottle.

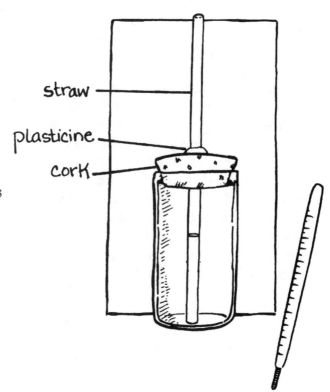

straw

plasticine

cork

6. Place the bottle and the thermometer in the pan of ice water, and make a pencil mark on the paper where the alcohol rises in the straw. Compare this with the temperature measured on the regular thermometer. Record this temperature by the mark on the paper.

7. Place the bottle and the thermometer in the pan of hot water, and record the temperature where the alcohol rises on the paper.

WHAT HAPPENED

The liquid inside the bottle **expanded** (got larger) when it was heated and **contracted** (got smaller) when it was cooled. The **molecules** (tiniest particles of a substance that keep all the properties of that substance) in a substance move more rapidly when heated and more slowly when cooled. Your home-made thermometer is not as reliable as a store-bought thermometer because it is open to the air and therefore affected by **air pressure** (the force the air puts on things). Air pressure is also called **barometric pressure**. To learn more about barometric pressure, see chapter 10.

DID YOU KNOW?

• The hottest temperature measured in the shade was 136°F (58°C) in Libya in 1922. The coldest temperature measured was −128°F (−89°C) in Antarctica in 1983.

CHAPTER 7
FUSION FRYER

A solar oven is a device that uses the sun's rays to cook food. Here are two easy ways to build a solar oven from recycled boxes. These ovens would come in handy if you were ever stuck on a desert island!

YOU WILL NEED

NOTE: Directions are given for two types of solar ovens. Build both so that you can compare their differences.

Shoe Box–Type Solar Oven

shoe box

scissors

ruler

Canister-Type Solar Oven

empty, round potato chip canister with shiny silver lining

knife (to be used only by an adult)

cardboard

adult helper

For Both Types of Solar Oven

aluminum foil

masking tape

2 ice cream sticks

sunscreen

sunglasses

hat

2 skewers

4 hot dogs

4 marshmallows

4 small potatoes

timer

black paper

helper

To Make the Shoe Box–Type Solar Oven:

1. Completely line the inside of the shoe box and its lid with aluminum foil, shiny side up. Use masking tape to hold the foil in place. The smoother the foil, the better your oven will work.

2. Make a reflector by using the scissors to cut a flap in the lid, 1 inch (2.5 cm) from the edge on three sides of the lid, then fold the reflector back. Tape the edges of the opening to keep the foil in place.

3. Place the lid on the foil-lined box, and tape the reflector to the ice cream stick. Use the stick to prop the reflector open.

To Make the Canister-Type Solar Oven:

1. Have an adult use the knife to cut an opening in the side of the round canister.

2. To make a reflector, cover a piece of cardboard with foil, then tape it to the side of the opening.

3. Use an ice cream stick to prop the reflector open, as you did for the other oven.

To Use the Ovens:

CAUTION: Put on sunscreen, sunglasses, and even a sun hat to keep the harmful rays of the sun off you. Never look directly into the sun.

1. Place the ovens in a sunny spot. Point the reflectors toward the sun so that its rays are directed into the ovens.

2. Skewer a hot dog and hold it in the center of the cooker. Have a friend do the same thing with the other cooker. Make note of which oven cooks a hot dog faster.

3. Repeat the experiment using a marshmallow. Make note of which oven cooks a marshmallow faster.

4. Put a raw potato in each oven and leave both in the sun for several hours. Make note of whether or not either oven cooks a potato.

5. Line the bottom of each oven with black paper, and repeat steps 2 through 4. Observe any differences.

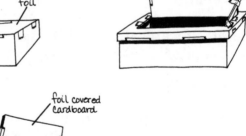

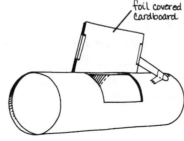

WHAT HAPPENED

Both solar ovens worked on the same principle: **radiant energy** (energy created by the sun or other source of light). The reflector directed the rays of the sun through the opening. The rays then bounced off the aluminum foil so that they were directed into a smaller space. When the sun's energy was **concentrated** (gathered together) in one area, the temperature inside the oven rose. The hottest spot in the oven was the spot where all the light rays **converged** (came to one point). The canister-type oven probably cooked the food faster than the shoe box–type, because curved surfaces reflect radiant energy better than surfaces with corners. The black paper did not reflect the sun's energy. The food did not warm up in the oven containing black paper. The oven itself warmed up slightly as the black paper absorbed the sun's energy.

DID YOU KNOW?

- If people in warm countries cooked with solar ovens, there would be less **deforestation** (removal of trees from forested areas), less **soil depletion** (loss of nutrients from the soil), and less **air pollution** (poisoning of the air by man-made substances) in their countries. Energy from the sun is free and clean. Solar ovens produce no smoke and need no electricity. You can even recycle materials to construct a solar oven.

- Solar ovens can be used to make terrific baked apples. In the middle of a large piece of aluminum foil, place apple slices, brown sugar, raisins, cinnamon, and margarine or butter. Fold the foil to hold the ingredients together, then cook them in the solar oven. Enjoy!

CHAPTER 8
GIVE IT A WHIRL

In science stores and some toy stores, you may have seen something called a **radiometer**. This instrument is used to measure the intensity of radiant energy. It looks like a light bulb with a small fan with black and silver blades. You can make your own radiometer, using simple materials found around your home.

YOU WILL NEED

two ½-by-2-inch (1-by-5-cm) strips of heavy-duty aluminum foil

glue

toothpick

matches (to be used only by an adult)

candle

10-inch (25-cm) piece of string or thread

pencil or straw

glass jar

adult helper

WHAT TO DO

1. Fold each strip of foil into the shape of a V. Glue the two V-shaped pieces to the toothpick at the folds so that they look like an X when viewed from the top. These pieces are the four blades of the radiometer.

2. Have an adult light the candle and use the flame to blacken every other blade of the radiometer. Be careful not to burn the toothpick.

3. Glue one end of the string to the toothpick. Tie the other end of the string around the center of the pencil or straw.

4. Place the pencil over the mouth of the glass jar, and suspend the radiometer blades in the jar. Wrap the string around the pencil to adjust the height. The blades should be able to move freely.

5. Place the radiometer in a sunny place, and watch what happens.

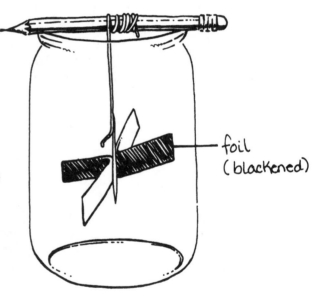

foil
(blackened)

WHAT HAPPENED

The blades began to spin. The blackened foil absorbed the heat, while the shiny side reflected the heat. Air particles bounced off the warmer blackened side at a faster speed than they did off the cooler shiny side. This caused the blades to **rotate** (turn).

DID YOU KNOW?

- Most people think that you should wear white in summer because the white will reflect the heat more than dark colors, keeping you cooler. But many people in the Middle East wear long black robes in the desert. This is because, while black clothing may absorb heat faster than white clothing, it also loses heat faster than white clothing.

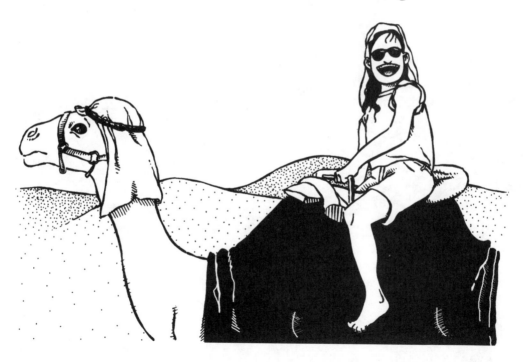

CHAPTER 9
STEAMED FRUIT

Have you ever wondered what you could do with a pineapple skin and an empty can of peanuts? Probably not. But aside from recycling these items, you can also make a steamboat out of them. Just wait till you see what it looks like!

YOU WILL NEED

pineapple

knife (to be used only by an adult)

spoon

nail

empty small, round peanut can with plastic lid

tap water

wooden skewers

bathtub or wading pool filled with water

small candle in metal holder

matches (to be used only by an adult)

adult helper

WHAT TO DO

1. Have an adult prepare the pineapple, as follows:

   • Cut a pineapple in half, from the leaves to the bottom of the fruit, then cut off the leaves.

   • Scoop out all the fruit from one half, leaving about ½ inch (1 cm) of rind. This will be your boat. Leave the skin someplace warm to dry overnight.

2. Have an adult use a nail to poke a small hole in the center of the plastic lid of the empty peanut can.

3. Fill the can about one-fourth full with water, and tightly close the lid.

4. After the pineapple has dried, poke two skewers through the skin about halfway from the top. The skewers should be far apart enough that the peanut can rests between them and high enough that the candle fits beneath them.

5. Place the boat in a bathtub filled with water.

6. Place the candle below the skewers, and have an adult light the candle.

7. Have an adult carefully rest the peanut can on its side over the candle, with the hole turned toward the back of the boat. Watch what happens.

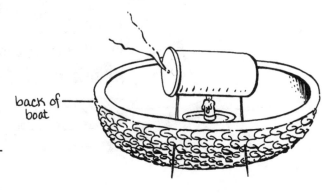

back of boat

WHAT HAPPENED

Your boat launched itself. The water in the peanut can boiled, creating **steam** (water in the form of a gas). The **steam pressure** (force caused by steam) built up inside the can and could only find a small hole to escape through. As the steam escaped through the hole in the back of the can, it pushed the boat forward.

DID YOU KNOW?

- It is more dangerous to get burned with steam than it is to be burned with hot water. Water boils to 212°F (100°C) and doesn't get hotter than that temperature. Steam can be heated to much higher temperatures. Steam has been used to power trains, boats, and the first cars. This type of power was **inefficient** (wasted energy) because so much heat escaped into the surrounding air, so other kinds of engines were developed.

PART III
EARTH SCIENCE

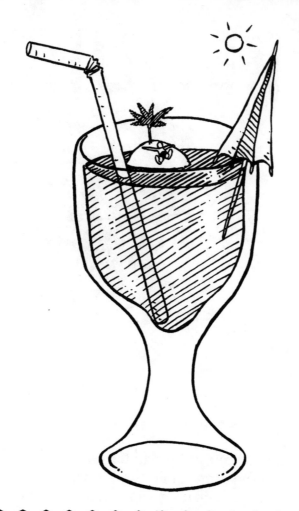

CHAPTER 10
GRACE UNDER PRESSURE

A barometer is an instrument that is used to forecast weather by measuring barometric pressure (the force the atmosphere, or air, puts on things). Here is a way of making your own barometer and learning what weather forecasters mean when they say, "The barometer is falling."

YOU WILL NEED

scissors

large balloon

large jar

rubber band

glue

straw

pen

3-by-5-inch (7.5-by-12.5-cm) index card

transparent tape

WHAT TO DO

1. Cut the balloon in half lengthwise so that you have a flat, round sheet of rubber.

2. Stretch the sheet of rubber over the mouth of the jar, and secure it with the rubber band.

3. Glue one end of the straw to the center of the sheet of rubber. The straw should lie on top of the rubber and extend over the rim of the mouth of the jar.

4. Make three marks on the long edge of the index card: the first mark in the center, the second mark between the center and one end, and the third mark between the center and the other end.

5. Tape the card to the side of the jar so that the marks face the straw and the center mark is even with the straw.

6. Place the jar in an area that has a constant temperature, and observe how the location of the straw changes.

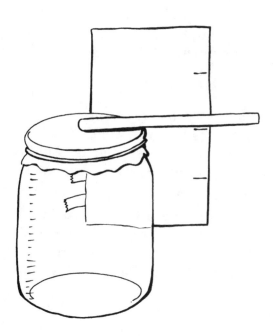

WHAT HAPPENED

The straw rose or fell, depending on the barometric pressure. When the barometric pressure outside the jar was higher than that inside the jar, it pushed the balloon down, making the straw rise. When the barometric pressure outside the jar was lower than that inside the jar, the balloon bulged out and the straw fell. Your homemade barometer is not as reliable as a store-bought barometer because it is affected by changes in temperature. It can be made more reliable by keeping it in an area where the temperature does not change much.

DID YOU KNOW?

- Falling barometric pressure often indicates that the weather will be worse. The pressure is usually higher on dry, clear days and lower on wet, cloudy days.

- Barometric pressure is measured in kilopascals (kPa) or millibars (mb). Normal barometric pressure at sea level is 101.32 kPa or 1013.2 mb.

CHAPTER 11
HERE COMES THE SUN

If you didn't have a watch, how could you tell time? You could use a **sundial,** which tells time according to the position of the shadow cast by a marker. For thousands of years people have been using the sun to tell time. Sundials need no batteries, are generally accurate no matter where you are in the world, and never need winding. The only problem is that they cannot tell time on cloudy days or at night.

YOU WILL NEED

modeling clay (plasticine)

small flowerpot

chopstick or wooden skewer

ruler

pencil

watch

WHAT TO DO

1. Place a small amount of modeling clay in the bottom of the flowerpot.

2. Push the chopstick into the clay so that it stands upright. The chopstick should stand about 3 inches (7.5 cm) above the rim of the pot.

3. At sunrise, put the pot in a place outdoors that is sunny all day, and locate the spot on the rim of the pot where the shadow is cast by the chopstick. Make a mark on this spot, and write the time by this mark.

4. Being careful not to move the pot from this position, mark the spot where the shadow is cast at each hour of the day till sunset.

5. Leave the pot in this position in order to tell time by the shadow.

WHAT HAPPENED

As the Earth rotated, it changed position relative to the sun. This caused the shadow of the chopstick to travel around the rim of the flowerpot. The shadow will remain in approximately the same place at the same time each day. The length of the shadow will change as the days become longer in summer or shorter in winter. Sundials are still made and used. To make them completely accurate, the part that casts the shadow is pointed toward Polaris, or the North Star (in the Northern

Hemisphere). This reference point is used because, as the Earth rotates, the North Star does not appear to change position in the sky with the passing seasons. Sundials will only work at the **latitude** (distance from the Earth's equator, the imaginary line running east to west around the globe) for which the sundial was designed.

DID YOU KNOW?

• Although sundials and clocks both tell time, they don't do so in the same way. Sundials tell the time by the position of the sun. Clocks tell the time in your time zone. Noon on a sundial is the point at which the sun passes the **meridian** (high point). Morning hours are called A.M., which stands for *ante meridiem* (before noon, or before the sun is at the high point). Afternoon hours are called P.M., which stands for *post meridiem* (after noon, or after the sun is at the high point).

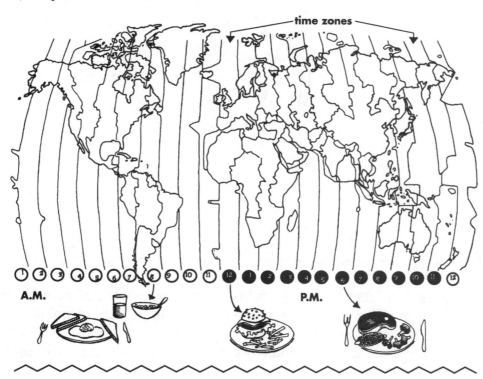

A.M.   P.M.

43

CHAPTER 12

WATER, WATER EVERYWHERE

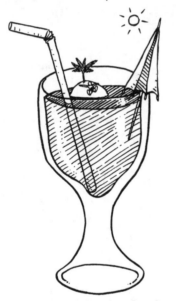

Remember that desert island from the solar oven experiment (chapter 7)? Well, what would happen if you were marooned on this island and there wasn't any fresh water to drink? How would you survive? If you knew how to remove the salt from ocean water, you'd be fine. In the unlikely event that this should ever happen to you, here's how to make fresh water.

YOU WILL NEED

large, deep metallic or glass bowl (taller than the mug)

boiling water (to be used only by an adult)

3 tablespoons (75 ml) of salt

food coloring

heavy glass mug or small glass jar

clean marbles, nuts, bolts, or other small, heavy objects

plastic wrap

timer

adult helper

WHAT TO DO

1. Have an adult fill a large bowl about one-third full with boiling water.

2. Add the salt to the water.

3. Add a few drops of food coloring to the salt water.

4. Place the mug in the center of the bowl of salt water, making sure that no water splashes inside the mug. If the mug does not sit flat, place some of the clean marbles inside it to weigh it down.

5. Tightly cover the large bowl with plastic wrap.

6. Place marbles in the center of the plastic wrap so that they pull the plastic wrap down over the opening of the mug.

7. Watch as the steam rises, collects on the plastic wrap, and flows into the mug.

CAUTION: Do not touch the bowl until the water has cooled.

8. When the bowl is cold (after about 1 hour), remove the plastic wrap and take out the mug. Taste the water inside the mug. Is it salty? What color is it?

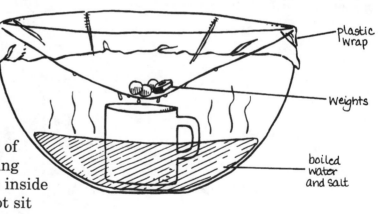

plastic wrap

weights

boiled water and salt

WHAT HAPPENED

The water inside the mug did not taste salty. It was also free of any coloring. This is because the salt and food coloring molecules **evaporated** (changed from a liquid to a gas) at a higher temperature than the water molecules. When the **water vapor** (water in the form of a gas, or steam) rose, it left the salt and food coloring in the bowl. The water vapor collected on the plastic wrap, where it **condensed** (changed from a gas to a liquid). The drops of water then fell into the mug. The process of removing salt from water is called **desalination**.

DID YOU KNOW?

- Many countries do not have a great deal of freshwater. These countries, such as Kuwait and Saudi Arabia, are located near seas, which contain salt. They have begun creating freshwater from seawater using giant **desalination plants** (industrial facilities where seawater is changed into freshwater by a process of evaporation and condensation). Even people in Canada and the United States sometimes have freshwater shortages. We can help by not wasting water in our daily lives. Don't leave the water running while brushing your teeth. Take a shower instead of a bath.

CHAPTER 13
ANTIGRAVITY DEVICE

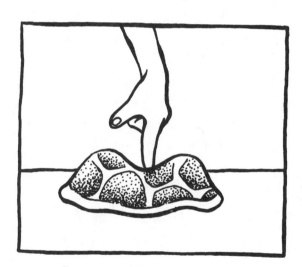

Many toy stores sell small plastic domes that jump into the air when they are inverted. Here's a simple way to make a giant "popper" and at the same time recycle an old handball.

YOU WILL NEED

old handball or squash ball that has lost its
  bounce

scissors or sharp knife (to be used only by an
  adult)

marking pen

vise

sandpaper or file

adult helper

WHAT TO DO

1. Have an adult make a dome out of the ball by using the scissors or knife to cut the ball in half, using the seam as a guide. If you can't find the seam, make a guide by drawing a line around the middle of the ball. Use a vise to hold the ball in place while cutting. The rubber should be at least ¼ inch (0.5 cm) thick.

2. Smooth out any rough edges on the dome by rubbing the cut edges over sandpaper. If you are using a ball that was torn, use the undamaged half.

3. Holding the dome curved side up in both hands, use your thumbs to turn the ball inside out. Pinch the top of the dome to hold it in place.

4. Quickly place the inverted dome, curved side up, on a flat surface, such as a tiled or wooden floor.

CAUTION: Do not stand directly over the ball!

5. Watch what happens.

6. Repeat the experiment on different surfaces, such as a carpet or concrete.

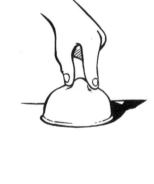

WHAT HAPPENED

After a short time, the dome snapped into the air, making a loud popping noise. The rubber dome is **elastic:** It goes back to its original shape after being deformed. As it turned inside out, the dome pushed down against the ground, causing it to bounce upward. The force of elasticity was so great that it was able to overcome the force of **gravity** (the force that pulls objects toward large objects, like the Earth), so the dome snapped into the air. When this happened, it created a partial **vacuum** (absence of air molecules) under the dome. As the dome left the ground, the vacuum was gradually broken and air molecules began to move under the dome around the edges. This caused the popping sound. This is much like the noise made when you put your finger in your mouth, suck your lips together to create a vacuum, then pop your finger out the side of your mouth. The experiment did not work as well on carpet or concrete, because the dome did not create as strong a vacuum on these surfaces.

DID YOU KNOW?

- Balls don't bounce in sand or if dropped from a low height. Balls bounce because they are made of elastic materials that allow them to have **kinetic energy** (energy of moving objects). Kinetic energy is put into a ball by you. To make a ball bounce, you must drop it from a great enough height that kinetic energy can build up in the ball. Also, the ball must hit a hard enough surface that the kinetic energy is kept in the ball rather than absorbed by the surface. Sand is not hard enough for a ball to be bounced on it. If you hit the sand several times with a ball, the energy will be absorbed by the sand molecules, causing them to move faster. Their movement will cause the sand to warm up a little.

PART IV
CHEMISTRY

CHAPTER 14
HI-HO SILVER

You've probably never helped your parents clean silver, but here's a fun and scientific way to do so. You'll be amazed at how well it works.

YOU WILL NEED

aluminum foil

plastic or enamel dishpan

½ cup (125 ml) of washing soda (available at a grocery store)

warm tap water

spoon

dirty silver items, such as spoons, trays, coffee urns, or old coins

timer

dish towel

WHAT TO DO

1. Place a large piece of aluminum foil in the bottom of the dishpan.

2. Pour the washing soda over the foil.

3. Fill the dishpan halfway with warm water, and stir to dissolve the soda.

4. Drop in dirty silver items, and allow them to sit for several minutes.

5. When the items look clean, remove them from the dishpan, then rinse and dry them.

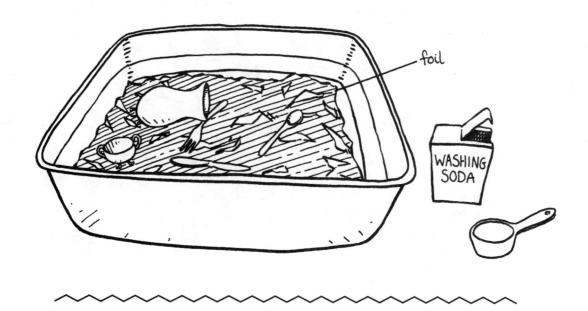

foil

WASHING SODA

WHAT HAPPENED

The silver was cleaned, but the aluminum foil lost its shine. Silver is an **element** (a pure substance that cannot be broken down chemically). When silver comes in contact with chemicals in the air, a **chemical reaction** (process of changing a substance into another substance) takes place. The silver and the chemicals react to form a **compound** (substance formed from two or more elements) called **tarnish** (the dirty film on the surface of the silver). When the silver was put into the water with the washing soda and aluminum foil, very tiny, electrically charged particles called **electrons** were drawn from the foil to the tarnish. This changed the tarnish back to shiny silver. The loss of electrons from the aluminum foil caused it to become discolored. The two processes occurred simultaneously. The gaining of electrons is called **reduction**, and the loss of electrons is called **oxidation**. Scientists call this electrical process in which electrons are transferred from one substance to another a **redox reaction**. The word *redox* comes from the two processes *red*uction and *ox*idation. To learn more about electrons, see chapter 20. To learn more about oxidation, see chapter 17. To learn more about redox reactions, see chapters 16 and 20.

DID YOU KNOW?

- Silver is a substance called a **metal**. All metals have certain properties in common: Metals are **lustrous** (shiny). Metals are also **malleable**, which means they can be beaten into thin, flexible sheets. Metals are good **conductors** of heat and electricity, which means they allow electricity and heat to pass through them. Metals are also **ductile**, which means they can be pulled into long, thin wires.

CHAPTER 15
SOFT SOAK

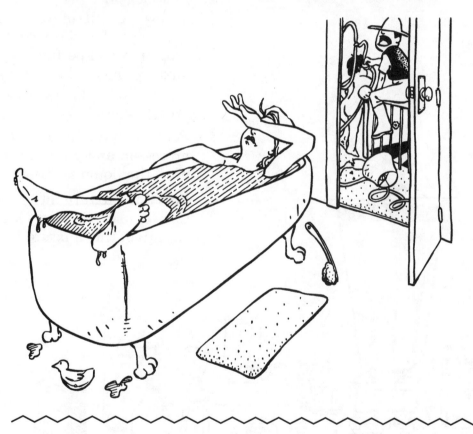

Do you have to be coaxed, bribed, or threatened before you will take a bath? By making your own bath products, you might be more anxious to participate in the cleansing ritual. The product of the following experiment is also a great gift to make and give to friends or relatives.

YOU WILL NEED

2 cups (500 ml) of baking soda or washing soda (available at a grocery store)

food processor or blender

measuring cup

warm tap water

food coloring

eyedropper

perfume

spoon

pretty bottles

adult helper

WHAT TO DO

1. Have an adult place baking soda in a food processor. Pulse the soda on low speed until it is a fine powder.

2. In a measuring cup, mix together 2 cups (500 ml) of warm water, a few drops of food coloring, and a drop or two of perfume to create a mixture that looks and smells wonderful. Stir until the liquid is evenly colored.

3. Pour the liquid into the food processor, and pulse the mixture until the liquid is absorbed.

4. Pour the mixture into pretty bottles. To use, add about ¼ cup (75 ml) of this mixture to the bath.

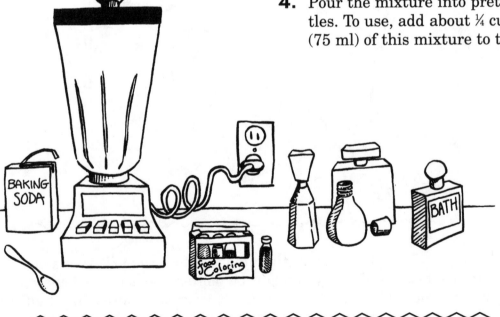

WHAT HAPPENED

You made bath salts. The soda or salts used in this experiment were compounds. Baking soda is sodium bicarbonate, while washing soda is a compound called sodium carbonate. Each of these compounds is made from a metal (sodium) and nonmetals (carbon, oxygen, and hydrogen). Compounds made from a metal and nonmetals are called **chemical salts**. When bath salts are added to the bath, they react with some of the minerals in the water, making the water feel "soft." Water that contains a lot of minerals is called "hard" water. Soap will also react with these minerals, so you must use much more soap in hard water than in soft water.

DID YOU KNOW?

• Lye is a compound, either sodium hydroxide or potassium hydroxide, that is used to make soap. Lye is **caustic** (capable of eating away the skin), but when it reacts to form soap, it is no longer caustic.

• Today nearly everyone buys soap, but many years ago, people made their own soaps using animal fat and lye. Soap can still be made from just about any fats, oils, or greases. The process of making soap is called **saponification**.

CHAPTER 16
A CUTE EXPERIMENT

How about using chemistry to clean your old pennies so that they look new? This is one experiment that really makes cents.

YOU WILL NEED

2 cups (500 ml) of vinegar

½ cup (125 ml) of salt

bowl

spoon

dirty pennies

water

dishtowel

WHAT TO DO

1. Put the vinegar and salt in a bowl, and stir.

2. Drop the dirty pennies into the bowl, then watch them change color.

3. When the pennies are shiny, remove them from the bowl, rinse them in water, and dry them with a towel.

CAUTION: Make sure you wash your hands after handling the pennies.

WHAT HAPPENED

The **acid** (sour-tasting chemical compound) in the vinegar reacted with the salt, removing the tarnish from the copper. This process is similar to the redox reaction between silver and aluminum foil in chapter 14. The *Cu* in the experiment's title refers to the **chemical symbol** (letters that stand for an element) for copper. Despite its color, chemists describe copper as a brown metal. The ancient Romans used copper for making many objects, and they named it after the island of Cyprus, where it was mined.

DID YOU KNOW?

- A little acid can clean copper, but too much acid can destroy copper. The acid in **acid rain** (rain that has reacted with the acid gases produced by air pollution) is eating away copper statues and parts of buildings around the world.

- Copper on older buildings and statues, such as the Statue of Liberty, is sometimes a greenish-blue color. Copper naturally turns this color by slowly reacting with chemicals in the air. This attractive green film is called a **patina.** Artists can artificially produce patinas more quickly by applying special chemicals that react with copper and rain to turn the copper object this color.

CHAPTER 17

HOT SHOTS PART TROIS

If you have ever watched an outdoor sporting event in the winter, or if you have spent any time in the cold, you have probably wished for a hand warmer. Here's an inexpensive way to make your own hand warmer.

YOU WILL NEED

1 tablespoon (15 ml) of fine iron filings

sealable plastic sandwich bag

¼ teaspoon (1 ml) of salt

1 tablespoon (15 ml) of fine vermiculite
(available from most garden shops)

1 teaspoon (5 ml) of tap water

WHAT TO DO

1. Place the iron filings in the bag.

2. Add the salt to the bag. Close the bag and shake it until the filings and salt are well mixed.

3. Open the bag and add the vermiculite. Reseal the bag and shake well.

4. When you are ready to use the hand warmer, add the water to the bag, then quickly reseal the bag. Hold the bag tightly between your hands, and squeeze it hard to mix everything together.

WHAT HAPPENED

After a minute or so, the bag began to feel warmer. You created a chemical reaction in the bag between the iron, salt, and a clear, odorless element in the water and air called **oxygen.** The iron was oxidized when it came into contact with the oxygen in the water and air. Adding salt helped to start the process of oxidation and also speeded it up. Oxidation produces heat, so it is said to be an **exothermic** reaction. The vermiculite acted as an **insulator** to keep the heat in. If you want to reuse your hand warmer later, squish out all the air from the bag and tightly reseal it. To start the oxidation process again, open the bag to let air in, then tightly reseal the bag.

DID YOU KNOW?

- The oxidation of iron is called **rusting**.
- Vermiculite is made from three metals—aluminum, magnesium, and iron. It expands when it is heated or wet. Vermiculite is used for insulation because it holds in heat and therefore keeps homes warmer. The less heat that escapes, the less energy that is needed to warm the home. Vermiculite also holds in water, so it is used in potting soil mixes to keep the roots of potted plants moist.

63

CHAPTER 18
BABY LOVE

If you have a baby brother or sister around your house, you probably think that diapers have only one use. Wrong! Diapers make a great science magic experiment. This next project won't make your baby sibling disappear, but you'll be amazed at what does vanish.

YOU WILL NEED

disposable diaper (extra absorbent works best)

paper

3 Styrofoam cups

water

audience

WHAT TO DO

1. Slowly tear open an unused diaper. Peel back some of the lining, and poke around until you can see the crystals buried in the diaper.

2. Sprinkle the crystals over a piece of paper, trying not to get to get too much of the lining mixed in. One diaper contains about 1 tablespoon (15 ml) or more of crystals.

CAUTION: Do not put these crystals in your mouth!

3. Place the crystals in one of the Styrofoam cups.

4. You are now ready to perform a great disappearing act. Gather an audience and tell them you are going to make water disappear.

5. Line up the three Styrofoam cups. Pour a little water into one of the empty cups until it is about one-fourth full. Next, pour the water from the first cup into the cup that contains the crystals. Tell a joke to distract your audience as you pretend to pour the water from the crystal-filled cup into the third cup.

6. Ask the audience which cup contains the water. Turn the last cup upside down. Turn the first cup upside down. Finally, turn the second cup upside down. No water comes out of any of them!

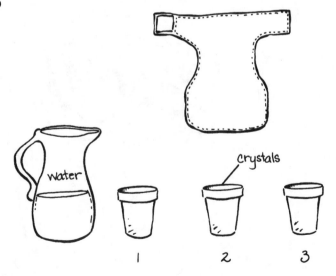

WHAT HAPPENED

The crystals absorbed the water. The crystals from the diaper are made from a chemical that can absorb large amounts of water. (This is how diapers keep babies dry.) The soaked crystals turned into a jellylike substance that stuck to the cup. The chemical does not harm babies when it is next to their skin.

DID YOU KNOW?

- Parents were bringing their babies in to doctors' offices because the babies had mysterious crystals on the surface of their diapers. The doctors were baffled by this strange condition! It turned out to be some of the tiny absorbent crystals, which had come out of the diaper onto the babies' skin.

CHAPTER 19
SHRUNKEN HEADS

In scary movies you sometimes see wrinkled shrunken heads. Pretty gross, huh! Here's a way to make your own shrunken head.

YOU WILL NEED

apple peeler (to be used only by an adult)

large apple

carving tools or paring knife (to be used only by an adult)

4 cups (1 liter) of tap water

mixing bowl

½ cup (125 ml) of salt

spoon

wire rack

paintbrushes

shellac or varnish

paint

beads

dressmaker's pins

glue

straw, string, or hair clippings

adult helper

WHAT TO DO

1. Have an adult peel the skin off an apple, then carve a face into the peeled apple using any carving tools or a paring knife.

2. Pour the water into a mixing bowl, then add the salt and stir well to dissolve the salt.

3. Place the apple in the bowl and leave it untouched for at least 24 hours.

4. Remove the apple and place it on a wire rack.

5. Leave the apple to dry in a warm place for 3 to 4 weeks.

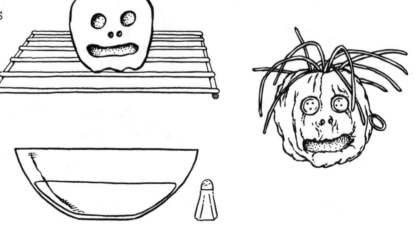

6. When the apple is dry, brush on a coat of shellac or varnish to seal the apple.

7. Decorate the apple.

- Color the face with paint.

- Attach beads with dressmaker's pins to make eyes.

- Make a mustache, eyebrows, and hair by gluing on straw, string, or hair clippings. Ask your hairdresser to let you have some of your own clippings for your shrunken head.

WHAT HAPPENED

The apple shrunk and became wrinkled. Apples contain water and salt. They can be preserved by adding more salt. This was done by placing the apple in a salt **solution** (uniform mixture of dissolved pure substances). The salt solution was **hypertonic** because it contained more salt than the apple. This is called having a higher **concentration** (degree to which a substance is in solution) of salt. After a while, the salt in the solution caused the water to leave the apple. This movement of liquid from an area of low concentration to an area of high concentration is called **osmosis**. When the amount of salt in the solution and in the apple was the same, the solution became **isotonic**. At this point, you removed the apple from the solution and placed it on a rack to dry. As the water in the apple evaporated, the salt was left behind, preserving the apple. The apple shrank as it lost its water by evaporation.

DID YOU KNOW?

- If the salt solution had contained a lower concentration of salt than the apple, it would have been a **hypotonic** solution.

- Your body uses osmosis every time you eat something. Water from the food you eat and drink passes through the walls of your intestine and travels through the blood to the cells of your body.

- You can "revive" apples, carrots, or potatoes that have become soft or wrinkled by placing them in ice water for about 10 minutes. Osmosis causes some of the water to enter the cells of the fruit or vegetable, making them plump and crunchy again.

PART V
ELECTRICITY AND MAGNETISM

CHAPTER 20
POWER
ARRANGERS

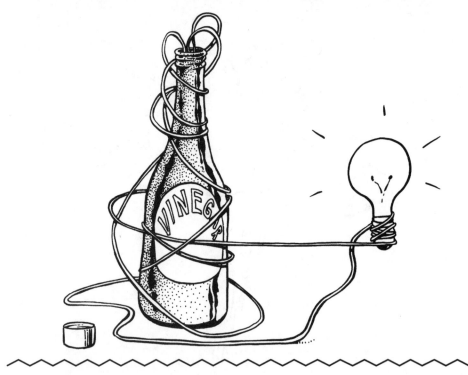

Did you ever think that the vinegar in your salad dressing could be used to turn on a light? Here's how to make it happen.

YOU WILL NEED

small glass jar

vinegar

LED (light emitting diode, available at most electronic components or hardware stores)

2 wires that have alligator clips on each end

zinc strip (available at most hardware or roofing supplies stores)

copper strip (or a copper tube or wire)

WHAT TO DO

1. Fill the jar with vinegar.

2. Spread apart the LED wires.

3. Use one of the alligator clip wires to connect the LED to the zinc strip by clipping one end to one of the LED wires and the other end to the zinc strip.

4. Use the other wire to connect the LED to the copper strip in the same way.

5. Place the free ends of the zinc strip and the copper strip in the vinegar, making sure that they do not touch.

WHAT HAPPENED

The LED lit up because it received an **electric current** (flow of electric charge). An electric charge occurs when tiny, negatively-charged particles called electrons move from one place to another. To make this happen, you set up an **electric circuit** (loop of conductive material through which an electric current can flow) that was connected to a **battery** (a device that uses chemicals to produce electricity). The battery con-

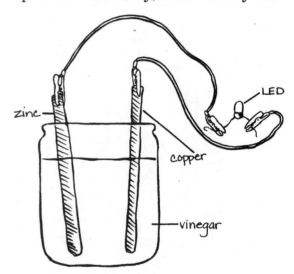

sisted of an **electrolyte solution** (a liquid that allows electrons to flow through it) and two **electrodes** (dissimilar metals capable of producing electricity between each other). The vinegar was the solution, and the zinc and copper were the electrodes. A redox reaction occurred. The zinc electrode attracted electrons from the solution, and the copper electrode gave up its electrons to the solution. The circuit allowed the buildup of electrons on the zinc electrode to travel through the wires to the copper. As the electrons traveled past the LED, the LED changed the electric energy to light energy, and the LED lit up.

DID YOU KNOW?

- A unit of electric energy is called a **volt** in honor of Alessandro Volta (1745–1827), who invented the first battery. He did this by taking disks of silver and zinc, placing fabric between them, and soaking them in an acid solution. He stacked these disks in alternating layers, then attached a wire to the top of the stack and a wire to the bottom of the stack. When he brought the ends of the two wires together, surprise! Sparks flew between the wires.

- It is dangerous to break open a store-bought alkaline battery, because it contains chemicals that are poisonous and can burn your skin.

CHAPTER 21
ZAPPED

Have you ever touched a metallic object after you ran around the house wearing wool socks? You probably received a shock. Read on to find out why.

YOU WILL NEED

hammer (to be used only by an adult)

nail (to be used only by an adult)

empty mayonnaise jar with lid

thick piece of wire or metal coat hanger

wire cutters (to be used only by an adult)

ruler

modeling clay (plasticine)

scissors

foil from a chewing gum or candy bar wrapper (with the paper removed)

transparent tape

4-inch (10-cm) square of aluminum foil

clear plastic disposable pen

wool sweater

paper towel

adult helper

WHAT TO DO

1. Have an adult use the hammer and nail to poke a hole through the center of the mayonnaise jar lid. Make sure the hole is big enough for the wire or coat hanger wire to fit through it.

2. Have an adult prepare the wire or coat hanger.

- If you are using a wire, use the wire cutters to cut a piece of wire that is 7½ inches (19 cm) long. Bend the wire so that it is in the shape of an L. There should be 1½ inches (4 cm) of wire on one side of the bend and 6 inches (15 cm) of wire on the other side.

- If you are using a coat hanger, use the wire cutters to cut the coat hanger on either side of one of the "elbows" to obtain a bent piece of wire that is 1½ inches (4 cm) long on one side of the elbow and 6 inches (15 cm) long on the other side. If wire cutters are not available, bend the coat hanger back and forth at these distances from the elbow until

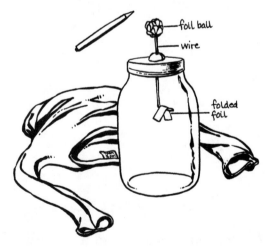

the wire breaks. Gently bend the wire at the elbow until it is in the shape of an L.

3. Remove the lid from the jar. Insert 2 inches (5 cm) of the long end of the wire through the hole in the lid so that the bend in the wire is below the lid. Secure the wire in place with modeling clay.

4. Cut the chewing gum foil into a 1-by-3½ inch (2.5-by-8.5-cm) strip. Fold the foil in half, bringing the short ends together.

5. Drape the folded foil over the short end of the wire and secure it with tape.

6. Carefully place the lid on the jar and screw it on.

7. Crumple the aluminum foil into a ball, then push it onto the exposed end of the wire, being careful not to push the wire into the jar.

8. Hold the pen in one hand and rub it with the sweater, then hold the pen close to the foil ball. Watch what happens to the foil inside the jar.

9. Repeat the experiment using a paper towel to rub the pen. Observe the difference in the amount of movement in the foil.

WHAT HAPPENED

The ends of the folded foil moved apart when the pen was held close to the foil ball. You created a **static charge** (an electric charge that stays in one place rather than flows in an electric current) in the pen by rubbing it against the wool sweater. A static charge can be caused by either an excess or a lack of electrons in the material that holds the charge. In this experiment, the pen had an excess of electrons. Some materials, such as wool (the sweater), tend to lose electrons when rubbed against materials that attract them, such as plastic (the pen). When the pen was placed close to the foil ball, the electrons traveled from the pen into the foil ball, through the wire, and down to the folded foil. The excess of electrons gave the folded foil a negative electric charge at both ends. The two ends of the foil moved apart because of a force called **repulsion**, which causes materials with the same electric charge to move apart. When you rubbed the pen with the paper towel, there was less movement of the foil. The paper does not lose electrons as easily as the wool. The device you created is called an **electroscope** because it detects an electric charge.

DID YOU KNOW?

• Lightning is caused by **static electricity** (electricity produced by a static charge). This occurs when low, heavy clouds called **cumulonimbus clouds** "rub" the air as they move through it. When enough static electricity has accumulated, one of two things can happen. If there is a nearby cloud with a different electric charge, cloud-to-cloud lightning will occur. If such a cloud is not nearby, cloud-to-ground lightning will occur. Lightning usually takes the shortest possible route to the ground. It will seek out tall objects, such as trees, telephone or metal poles, or metal objects. It will also be drawn toward bodies of water, such as ponds, lakes, or rivers. If you are ever caught in a lightning storm, stay away from tall objects and bodies of water. Find a low spot and stay close to the ground, or remain in your car. Lightning *can* strike twice in the same place.

Chapter 22
To Catch a Thief

Do you ever wonder if your younger brother or sister is sneaking up on you? Wouldn't you love to have some advance warning? Here's a way to build your own burglar alarm.

YOU WILL NEED

scissors

two 6-by-6-inch (15-by-15-cm) pieces of
corrugated cardboard

masking tape

aluminum foil

three 1-foot (30-cm) pieces of electrical wire

wire strippers (to be used only by an adult)

size D battery

electric buzzer (available from electronic
components stores)

adult helper

WHAT TO DO

1. Cut a 4-by-4-inch (10-by-10-cm)
   square out of the center of the first
   6-by-6-inch (15-by-15-cm) piece of
   cardboard and discard it.

2. Tape aluminum foil over the
   square hole.

3. Completely cover one side of the
   second piece of cardboard with foil,
   extending the foil onto the back of
   the cardboard. Secure the foil with
   tape.

4. Tape the two pieces of cardboard
   together so that the foil square is
   exposed and the foil on the second
   piece is concealed.

5. Have an adult remove the insulation from the ends of all three
   pieces of wire with the wire
   strippers.

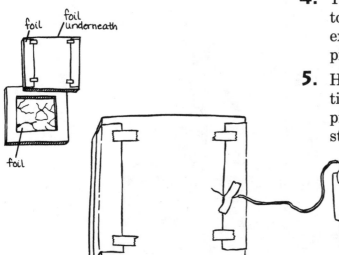

6. Tape one end of the first wire to the edge of the second piece of cardboard. Tape the other end of this wire to the positive terminal of the battery.

7. Tape the second wire to the edge of the foil square and to the positive wire of the buzzer.

8. Tape the third wire to the negative wire of the buzzer and to the negative terminal of the battery.

9. Place the burglar alarm under a throw rug near your door so that the foil square touches the floor. Wait to see what happens when someone steps on the rug.

WHAT HAPPENED

When someone stepped on the rug, the buzzer sounded. You made an alarm that is operated by a simple **switch** (a device for making or breaking the connection in an electric circuit). The wires running from the foil to the buzzer and battery created an electric circuit. When someone stepped on the rug, the two pieces of foil touched, working as a switch to turn the alarm on. An electric current traveled from the battery to the buzzer, causing the alarm to sound.

DID YOU KNOW?

Household alarms on windows and doors typically operate as simple electric circuits. The alarm sounds if you break the circuit by opening the window or door. The burglar alarm you made operates in the opposite way—the alarm sounds when the circuit is completed instead of when it's broken.

CHAPTER 23
DIMMER DEMENTIA

Have your parents ever told you to turn down the volume? While most children aren't created with a switch that will make them quieter, most electric noisemakers are. Here's a project you can do to see how they work.

YOU WILL NEED

knife (to be used only by an adult)

wooden pencil

3 electrical wires with alligator clips on the ends

6-volt battery

LED from electronic components or hardware store

adult helper

WHAT TO DO

1. Have an adult use the knife to carefully strip all the wood from one side of the pencil so that all of the pencil lead is exposed on that side of the pencil.

2. Connect one of the alligator clips of the first wire to one end of the pencil lead and the other alligator clip of this wire to either terminal of the 6-volt battery.

3. Connect one of the alligator clips of the second wire to the other terminal of the battery and the other alligator clip of this wire to one wire of the LED.

4. Connect one of the alligator clips of the third wire to the other wire of the LED.

5. Slide the other alligator clip of the third wire back and forth along the pencil lead.

WHAT HAPPENED

The light given off by the LED got brighter or dimmer, depending on the point at which the third wire made contact with the pencil lead. Because pencil lead is not a really good conductor, more electric current flowed through the LED when only a short section of pencil lead was included in the circuit. This made the light from the LED brighter.

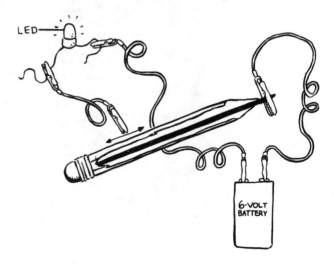

DID YOU KNOW?

- Many homes have a light switch that operates in the same way as the dimmer switch in this experiment. The part in the light switch that acts to control the amount of electricity flowing through a circuit is called a **rheostat.** Rheostats are also found in electric stoves, refrigerators, microwaves, and the volume switches on radios.

CHAPTER 24
CALLING ALL SCIENTISTS

If you have teenage brothers or sisters, you know how much time they spend on the telephone. Don't you wish you had your own phone line to call your friends? You can make your own simple phone by using common household items.

YOU WILL NEED

sharp pencil

empty matchbox without the sleeve

3 pieces of very thick pencil lead from a
mechanical pencil

sandpaper

2 pieces of insulated electrical wire, long
enough to go between two rooms in your
house

1-foot (30-cm) piece of wire

wire strippers (to be used only by an adult)

masking tape

size D battery

earphone (from a portable radio or tape
player)

adult helper

WHAT TO DO

1. Have an adult use the pencil to
poke two holes on each short end of
the matchbox. The holes should be
parallel to each other, and close to
the bottom of the box.

2. Gently rub the pencil leads from
top to bottom with the sandpaper.
Push the first pencil lead in one
hole and out the opposite hole so
that the same amount of lead
sticks out either side of the box. Do
the same in the other hole. Lay the
third piece of pencil lead inside the
box, across the first two pieces of
lead.

3. Have an adult remove the insulation from the ends of the wires
with wire strippers.

4. Tape one end of the short wire to
either terminal of the battery and
wind the other end around the end
of one pencil lead.

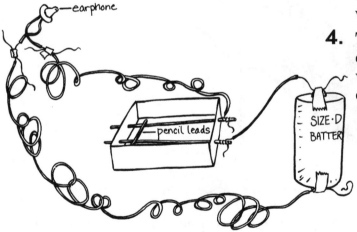

86

5. Have an adult use the wire strippers to remove the jack from the earphone. Spread the earphone wires apart.

6. Wind one end of the first long wire around the other pencil lead, and tape the other end of the wire to one of the earphone wires.

7. Tape one end of the second long piece of wire to the other earphone wire, and connect the other end of the wire to the other terminal end of the battery. You have completed a circuit.

8. Have a friend carefully carry the earphone to another room, making sure all wires stay attached. Holding the matchbox with two fingers on the long sides of the box, speak into the box.

WHAT HAPPENED

When you spoke into the box, the sound of your voice caused the bottom of the box to **vibrate** (move back and forth). These vibrations were carried to the pencil leads, which also vibrated and changed the electric current in the wire slightly. The electric current variations traveled through the wire and caused the earphone to vibrate, making sounds that your friend could hear.

DID YOU KNOW?

• Telephones are now used not only for speaking to others, but also to send and receive information from computers and fax machines. An **optical scanner** is used in every fax machine. This device "reads" a printed page, then sends information about the page through the telephone line to a fax machine. The fax machine then interprets the information and prints the page.

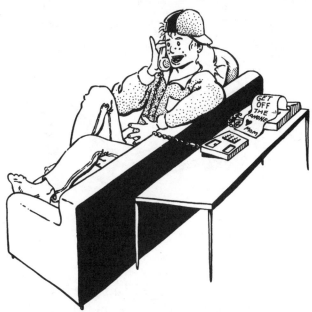

CHAPTER 25
PICK ME UP

How big a magnet would you need to pick up a car? Here's a way to make a magnet strong enough to pick up metal objects, and clever enough to put them back down.

YOU WILL NEED

5 feet (2 m) of insulated electrical wire

long iron or steel nail

wire strippers (to be used only by an adult)

masking tape

size D battery

compass

metallic objects (such as diaper pins, paper clips, and pins)

pencil lead

adult helper

WHAT TO DO

1. Tightly wrap the wire around the nail, leaving at least 1 foot (30 cm) of wire at either end. Have an adult use the wire strippers to strip the insulation off a small section of each end of the wire.

2. Tape one end of the wire to the positive terminal of the battery and the other end to the negative terminal of the battery. Make sure there is a good connection between the metal of the battery terminals and the wire.

3. Hold the coiled nail near the compass. In which direction does the compass needle point?

4. Hold the coiled nail near different metallic objects. See how many objects the nail can pick up before it won't hold any more.

5. Disconnect the wires from the battery. Watch what happens to the objects.

6. Unwrap the nail to see whether the bare nail can pick up anything metallic.

7. Hold the uncoiled nail near the compass. Watch what happens.

8. Repeat the experiment, using the pencil lead. Observe any differences between the pencil lead and the nail.

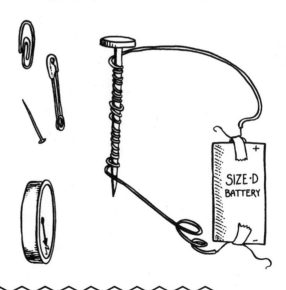

WHAT HAPPENED

You made an **electromagnet**. This type of magnet uses an electric current to produce **magnetism** (the attraction of iron to a magnet). An electromagnet consists of a source of electricity (the battery) and a **solenoid** (the coiled wire). The magnetic force of a magnet causes the particles of iron substances to line up. The nail was able to be magnetized because it is made of a mixture of metals, including iron. When the nail was disconnected from the battery, the large objects fell off the nail as it began to lose its magnetism. The nail was weakly magnetic, so it was able to pick up small objects. The pencil lead was not able to become magnetized. Pencil lead does not contain iron; it is a form of carbon called graphite. A compass works by aligning its needle with the magnetic field of the Earth, which makes the needle point north. The compass needle was drawn toward the electromagnet because the magnetic field of the electromagnet was stronger than the magnetic field of the Earth. The magnetized nail had less effect on the compass. Electromagnets can be made very strong by increasing the amount of electric current. When an old car is about to be compacted, or packed together, for scrap metal, a huge electromagnet picks up the car and puts it in the compactor.

DID YOU KNOW?

• Trains in North America are usually powered by diesel or electricity. One of the biggest energy drains on trains is **friction**, a force that occurs when the wheels rub against the metal tracks. Trains also lose energy by pushing against the air in front of them. This **air resistance** (resistance to air pressure) can be reduced by making the train a sleeker shape. These **aerodynamic** (designed to reduce air resistance) trains are called "bullet trains" because they look like bullets when viewed from the front. Unlike traditional trains, bullet trains use a type of track that has a magnetic charge. The train and the track have the same magnetic charge, which makes them repel each other slightly. The train rises slightly above the track. This reduces friction and allows the train to travel at higher speeds than traditional trains.

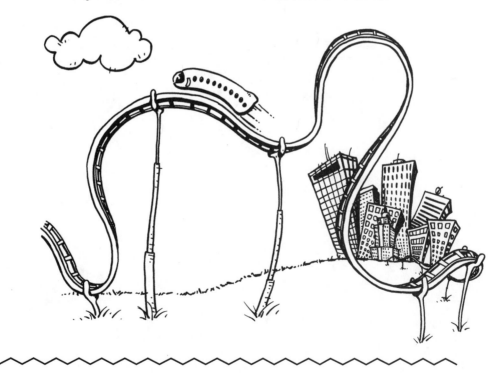

GLOSSARY

absorb To take in.

acid A sour-tasting chemical compound that can eat away other materials.

acid rain Rain that has reacted with the acid gases produced by air pollution.

aerodynamic Designed to reduce air resistance.

air pollution Poisoning of the air by man-made substances.

air pressure The force that air puts on things. Also called **barometric pressure**.

air resistance Resistance to air pressure.

astronomer A scientist who studies objects in the sky.

astronomical Relating to the stars and planets.

barometer An instrument used to forecast weather by measuring barometric pressure.

barometric pressure The force the atmosphere, or air, puts on things.

battery A device that uses chemicals to produce electricity.

camera obscura A darkened box with a pinhole at one end that allows light to enter and cast an upside-down image at the other end of the box.

caustic Capable of eating away the skin.

chemical reaction The process of changing a substance into another substance.

chemical salts A compound containing a metal and nonmetals.

chemical symbols Letters that stand for elements.

compound A substance formed from two or more elements.

concentrate To gather together in one area.

concentration The degree to which a substance is in solution.

condense   To change from a gas to a liquid.

conductor   A material that allows heat or electricity to pass through it.

contract   To get smaller.

converge   To come to one point.

cumulonimbus cloud   A low, heavy cloud.

deforestation   The removal of trees from forested areas.

desalination   The process of removing salt from water.

desalination plant   An industrial facility where seawater is changed into freshwater by a process of evaporation and condensation.

ductile   Capable of being pulled into long, thin wires.

elastic   Capable of returning to the original shape after being deformed.

electric circuit   A loop of conductive material through which an electric current can flow.

electric current   A flow of electric charge.

electrodes   Dissimilar metals capable of producing electricity between each other.

electrolyte solution   A liquid that allows electrons to flow through it.

electromagnet   A magnet that uses an electric current to produce magnetism.

electron   A very tiny particle with a negative electric charge.

electroscope   A device that detects an electric charge.

element   A pure substance that cannot be broken down chemically.

evaporate   To change from a liquid to a gas.

exothermic   Capable of producing heat through chemical reaction.

expand   To get larger.

focal length   The distance from a lens to the point where the image of an object can be focused.

friction   The force that occurs when objects move against each other.

gravity   The force that pulls things toward large objects like the Earth.

hypertonic   A solution having a higher concentration of dissolved substances than another solution.

hypotonic   A solution having a lower concentration of dissolved substances than another solution.

inefficient Wastes energy.

insulator A material that keeps heat in.

isotonic A solution having the same concentration of dissolved substances as another solution.

kaleidoscope A tube that has a peephole at one end and mirrors and pieces of shiny, colored materials at the other. When the tube is turned, the colored materials tumble and are reflected in the mirrors.

kinetic energy The energy of moving objects.

latitude The distance from the Earth's equator, the imaginary line running east to west around the globe.

lens A curved piece of clear glass or other transparent material that can focus or spread light rays.

lustrous Shiny.

magnetism The attraction of iron to a magnet.

magnify To enlarge.

malleable Easily beaten into a thin, flexible sheet.

meridian The highest point of the sun.

metal A substance that is **lustrous, malleable, conductive,** and **ductile.**

mirror image A reverse copy of an image.

molecule The tiniest particle of a compound that keeps all the properties of that compound.

optical illusion A misleading visual image.

optical scanner A device that "reads" a printed page, allowing for fax transmission.

osmosis The movement of liquid from an area of low concentration to an area of high concentration.

oxidation The process of losing electrons.

oxygen A clear, odorless element in water and air.

patina The attractive green film that forms on objects containing copper.

pinhole camera A camera that lets light enter through a small hole to expose film.

pollute To harm or poison the environment.

praxinoscope   A device that uses mirrors to reflect a series of pictures on the inside of a drum.

radiant energy   Energy created by the sun or other source of light.

radiometer   An instrument used to measure the intensity of radiant energy.

radio telescope   A huge telescope that looks like a satellite dish and that picks up radio waves from space.

radio waves   Waves of energy that can be picked up by a radio receiver.

recycle   To reuse materials rather than throw them away.

redox reaction   An electrical process involving the transfer of electrons from one substance to another.

reduction   The process of gaining electrons.

reflect   To give back light.

reflecting telescope   A telescope that uses curved mirrors instead of lenses not only to focus light but also to flip the image right side up.

refract   To bend light.

refracting telescope   A telescope that uses lenses to refract light and produce an upside-down image.

repulsion   The force that causes materials with the same electric charge to move apart.

rheostat   A device that controls the amount of electricity flowing through a circuit.

rotate   To turn.

rusting   The oxidation of iron.

saponification   The process of making soap.

scope   Any device that is used to look at things.

soil depletion   The loss of nutrients from the soil.

solar oven   A device that uses the sun's rays to cook food.

solenoid   The coiled wire in an electromagnet.

solution   A uniform mixture of dissolved pure substances.

spectrum   The colors of the rainbow.

static charge   An electric charge that stays in one place rather than flowing in an electric current.

static electricity   Electricity produced by a static charge.

steam   Water in the form of a gas. Also called **water vapor**.

steam pressure Force caused by steam.

stroboscopic effect The appearance of stopping or slowing the movement of a turning object.

sundial An instrument that tells time according to the position of the shadow cast by a marker.

switch A device for making or breaking the connection in an electric circuit.

tarnish The dirty film that forms on silver when it reacts with chemicals in the air.

telescope An instrument for looking at distant objects.

terrestrial Relating to Earth.

thermometer An instrument used for measuring temperature.

vacuum The absence of air molecules or other substances.

vibrate To move back and forth.

volt A unit of electric energy.

water vapor Water in the form of a gas. Also called **steam**.

wave A movement that repeats itself.

wavelength The distance between similar points on a wave.

zoetrope A device shaped like a cylinder with a slit in one side through which a series of pictures can be viewed.

INDEX

READER REPLY FORM

YOU CAN HELP US WRITE A BOOK!

Do you wonder how we come up with these experiments? Some of them come through hard work, some happen by accident, and some are from our friends and coworkers. Here's your chance to become an author. Have you got a favorite experiment or science fact? Have you done a science experiment in your classroom that made everyone say "wow!"? What did you do for a science fair? You can send us your favorite project and, if our editors are still speaking to us, we'll write a book with your special activities.

HERE'S HOW IT WORKS:

1. Try out your science experiment with an adult family member or a teacher.
2. Write what you did on a copy of the "Experiment" form.
3. Have an adult cosign the form.
4. Mail the form to us:

John Wiley & Sons Inc.
605 Third Ave.
New York, New York 10158-0012

Attention: Shar Levine / Leslie Johnstone
In care of Kate Bradford

EXPERIMENT

Name of Experiment _____

Materials You Need

_____

_____

_____

_____

_____

_____

What to Do

1. _____
2. _____
3. _____
4. _____
5. _____
6. _____
7. _____
8. _____
9. _____
10. _____

What Happened

_____

_____

_____

_____

_____

Experimenter's Name _____**Age** _____

Address_____

City _____**State/Province** _____**Country** _____

ZIP Code/Postal Code _____ **Phone Number (__)**_____

Parental Permission

I, _____, do hereby attest that_____

(experimenter's name) performed the above experiment. I give my permission to

print this experiment in a book. I understand that no personal information will be

released or printed in the book without my permission.

Date _____